tales
of a
recovering
love addict,

by shadress denise

other books by shadress denise

poetry....
Disturbia
hello. goodbye. never again
Liberated
Late Night Thoughts
Love, Heartbreak & Hangovers

novels....
Who Do You Love?
Who Do You Love Too?
Who Do You Love Now?
Smitten Kitten

acknowledgements

As I write this, I am in awe of where I am in life. I remember the first time I wrote the first poem starting this journey. My first book was *Broken Hearts, Renewed Spirits* and at the time, when I first began writing, I did it for therapy and nothing else. During those early years, I was simply expressing myself on paper. I had no idea I would become a writer, nor did I ever imagine I would be writing the acknowledgements to my tenth book! OMG, how time flies when you are doing what you love and are buried so deep inside of it you can't help but give it your all. This book, my tenth published book also solidifies my five-year anniversary in the publishing world. The month I was getting ready to turn thirty-one, it was as if I could hear God's voice clear as day saying to me, "Shadress it's time to publish your work." Now, I'm half way through my thirties, and I couldn't fathom this would be where I am.

When writing this book, I was like what am I going to call it? I needed something that would fit the ups and downs, back and forth, and this title seemed to fit just right. My original name (I'll be using for a later project) for some reason didn't fit anymore. It never captured the raw emotion of love and the heartache I needed it to convey. It's funny because I remember tossing back and forth with a title and nothing ever made sense, until it did. Tales of a Recovering Love Addict was the absolute perfect title and it fit perfectly to follow behind Love, Heartbreak & Hangovers. It marked my tenth book published and the eighth poetry book I had written so it had to show growth. It's like I need to say it out loud; "10 published books, 8 poetry books written, and 5 years as a published author." I'd like to say I'm proud of myself. I finally found a career I love, I'm passionate about, and I can utterly be myself in.

To those who hold this book in your hands, whether it's your first, third or tenth book you've read by me, THANK YOU! I humbly appreciate your support from the top, sides, and bottom of my heart. Without the love and support of family, friends, and readers this wouldn't be possible. I hope you enjoy reading this as much as I enjoyed writing it.

love and light,

shadress denise

experimentation...

the masks we wear | glass windows | window shopping | the devil made me do it | jailbreak | crossroads | the voices | paralyzed | my sponsor | cracked | lifeboat | final requests | traitor | make me believe again | russian roulette | the tyrant | clusterfuck | sobreity | bullshit truths | memories on my skin | binging | familiar strangers | emotionless regret | proof of life | signs of an addict | control | lose, lose | love drought | conundrum | mischief | premonition | a painting in vengeance | the debt for happiness | the natural bridge | what we reap | late night vices | purple is the sky | the taste of time | do you ever think of me? | the problem with temptation | compromises | the shaky sounds | reasons to stay | lies you tell on our pillows | eight months after | where we hide our wild things | internal orgasms | all the nameless | maybe you knew | focus

regular use...

whitewashed dreams | planted in pain | heal to tow | a house so empty | tell me where hope lives | a carnival of heathens | naked as the name | soundless downpours | no one arrived | sleeping with the lights on | false god | mood swings | 2 centimeters | trip wires and scotch tape | i know better now | layoff | perspective | steady | provoke | misstep | permission | hoarder | serendipity | crush | certainly, not me | collector's item | caught between a rock & a hard place | willpower | momentary highs | can't love me | lost cause | ignorance is bliss | moment of silence, please | sweet talker | lovers anonymous | the worst kind of love | séance | a question that bleeds | misdirection | truancy | hopeless romantic | taking bets | nine lives | confession |

risky use...

treehouse | got a broken heart again | let them leave | tragically beautiful | this is me letting you go | he wants to be a poem | i'm sorry i wasn't good enough | boundaries | breathing underwater |

suitcase | **delusions** | cautionary tale | **glimpse** | i'm just going to lie & tell you starting over was easy | **wasting time on temptation** | chasing secrets | **origin of bad habits** | the horizon is not a line | **hell in the holy city** | like deconstructed origami | **sunday coffee and second chances** | dead language, or learning to speak | **when the bottom falls out** | accidental birthdays | **the night we lost the moon** | flowers in my hair | **hiraeth** | counting backwards from 10 | **21st century bloodletters** | #yourefreeyourefreeyourefree | **relearning happiness** | games in which we rename everything | **white noise** | less like a flower, more like a sword | **balloons shaped like anchors**

dependence...

let's pretend i've never said this before | **surviving sadness** | we told secrets in parked cars | **ash in my veins** | born a bastard | **how to eat honeycomb** | your love is blue fire, red lies | **wishful thinking** | sacrificial kindness | **glimpse** | a memory i cannot forget | **calvin klein and menthol cigarettes** | all the things lost | **ghosts we no longer haunt** | broken dolls | **is forever real?** | today it hit me | **tell me how to heal** | love and other plagues | **to all the boys i've loved before** | the alchemist | **die in love, live forever**

...addiction

one of these days, I'm going
to get my shit together. I'm
going to stop overdosing on
toxic love, but until then.

the masks we wear

He's kissing me as
   if I mean something to him,
   and I know
   it's only because
   the fragrance I am wearing
   reminds him of her.
   the one he no longer speaks of,
   the space I am now filling.
   all in the name of love,
   all because of this burning need
   I have to be loved.

glass windows

I continue to sit here
   with you,
   wiping away the fingerprints,
   pain left behind and smears
   that are really small cracks
   in our life, in our lie,
   as denial builds
   a barrier between
   me and the pain
   I know is waiting
   for me on the other side
   when I face the fact, I let you
   break my heart *again*.

window shopping

Don't touch my soul
　　if you came here to do nothing
　　but manipulate
　　the happiness it dances to
　　and the peace it subsides in.
　　It can no longer afford
　　the currency of your chaos.

the devil made me do it

You climbed inside of me.
    You buried yourself within
    the layers of my skin.
    You filled me up with your love
    and in the blink of an eye—
    you snatched it all away.
    Now I'm here, shuffling through
    brokenness and naivety.
    Navigating through my love for you,
    and the compartmentalized hurt
    that now lives inside of me.
    Struggling to get over
    being addicted to love,
    and unsuccessfully,
    fighting this addiction to you.

jailbreak

This empty hole
    nestled within
    the middle of my chest
    is nothing more than
    a reminder of the betrayal
    my heart showed me
    when it left running after you,
    and I'm trying to decide
    if I should chase it
    or let it be free.

crossroads

I'm half past
    "fuck you, I don't care"
    and only moments away
    from crawling back to
    you screaming,
    "please don't leave me."
    I am stuck in this
    emotional purgatory
    and you have never been freer.

the voices

My heart whispers
 one thing
 about you,
 and my mind screams another.
 Either way,
 the memory of you won't die
 and it's slowly killing me.

paralyzed

The thought of you
    no longer moves me,
    and I'm not sure
    if I'm full of relief or regret.
    however, the numbness pardons
    my heart to what would be
    the unbearable pain
    of your absence.

my sponsor

He tried to convince me
    he was the only one
    who could inflame
    the light behind my eyes again.
    He told me how
    dark, and troubling life
    without him would be.
    (and I believed him).
    He made me believe
    he could make it all better,
    so, I gave him everything.
    All the broken pieces
    my heart was left in,
    the molecules of faith
    I had hidden from them.
    All the broken promises
    the other saviors left behind.

cracked

We take pieces from one another
  in hopes
  we can somehow repair
  what is broken inside us.
  But hurt can't fix hurt, and
  after all this time, nothing
  I have collected from you
  feels remotely close to
  making me feel complete,
  and I need to put myself
  back together without you
  before it's too late.

lifeboat

I am drowning in insecurities.
    Yours, mine, and the other people
    who have subsequently
    come and go.
    But no matter how hard
    I fight to hold on,
    nothing about this love
    can pull me to safety.

final requests

Blow out my candles baby,
 and make it count.
 My only wish
 is to feel your breath
 upon my skin this one last time
 before we say goodbye.

traitor

Hold my hand
　　as tight as you can.
　　My fingers don't know
　　you have
　　deceived my heart
　　and it has gone numb.

make me believe...again

Your lips spouted tales of wonder
    and the forever kind of life.
    But your eyes told a different story,
    the story I needed to believe,
    the story I wanted so badly to
    be true for you, for us.
    And I be damned if I didn't fall
    for the wrong tale once again.

russian roulette

Being in love with you
    is like letting you hold a
    loaded gun to my head.

    I know you can destroy
    my entire world with one shot,
    yet the curiosity of it all
    makes me want to pull the trigger,
    just to see if I will survive.

the tyrant

You keep your hand
    close to my heart.
    Not because you want to know
    what it feels like,
    but to let me know
    with one stroke, anarchy
    can be let loose within its walls.

clusterfuck

I am stuck between
    somewhere and nowhere,
    here and there.
    I am robust
    and still I have never
    felt so weak.
    I am full-bodied, though somehow,
    I have become diluted.
    I am a giant trapped
    in the frame of something so small.
    I hate you and I love you
    at the same time,
    I don't want you,
    but I need you,
    and that within itself
    is a mystery of feelings
    that will never make sense.

sobriety

Your calloused hands
  feel rough against my skin,
  and for a moment,
  fear strikes,
  and I ask myself if my heart
  is truly safe in this unknown place.
  Or will I, like the many before me
  slip through the cracks of your fingers
  and shatter into tiny,
  unrecognizable pieces.

bullshit truths

Happily ever after's
    love fables,
    and romantic anecdotes,
    that I drug myself with,
    that's what we have,
    that's all we'll ever have.
    Beguiled doses of forever
    we know will never come,
    infused with moments of today,
    and watered down
    versions of false hope,
    we persuade ourselves into believing
    will come tomorrow.
    This is what makes up our reality,
    our bullshit versions of truth.

memories on my skin

Maybe one day,
I'll be able to forget
the hurtful words you said,
and even the unholy things
you did to my body
I have yet to recover from.
Perhaps, one day
I won't remember
what you taste like.
but for now,
leave your words on my lips
and have your way with my mind.

binging

I'm finally on the edge of recovery
    and I need you to stick around
    this time.
    I need you to be absolutely sure
    this is where you want to be.
    because I'm not sure
    I can survive another one
    of your temporary returns.
    I can't guarantee I won't overdose
    on heartbreak & sadness.
    I am positive I'm not strong enough
    to survive another goodbye.

familiar strangers

Take what you must
 and be gone by the morning.
 I don't want my sheets
 or my skin to become
 too familiar with your scent.

emotionless regret

I'm glad you
    found someone to love
    you,
    but I'm not sorry
    it couldn't be me.

proof of life

The only time I know
    you're alive is when you grab
    my hand to keep me
    from walking out the door,
    and that's just
    not enough
    for my heart, anymore.

signs of an addict

I'm always missing people
> I shouldn't be missing,
> crying over people who
> don't deserve my tears,
> loving people my heart
> will eventually need
> to heal from.

control

You weakened the walls
of my heart,
but I didn't collapse.
I didn't fall apart
and I'm still here.
Breathing better
than I ever have before.
Better because I finally
freed my lungs of you.

lose, lose

You love me more
     when I am broken,
     so, I don't waste my time
     pretending
     to have it all together
     anymore.
     It's a win-win for the both of us.

love drought

You're secretly suicidal
    and I am silently depressed,
    yet we sit here holding on
    to the faint sound of a heartbeat
    that is slipping away.
    We participate in this craziness because
    we are terrified of facing the truth.
    The reality that we know
    we are no good for one another,
    all so we can drain each other,
    take all that's left,
    and suffer together.

conundrum

I stare at the puzzle pieces of my life
      in front of me,
      connected, but just barely,
      and I realize I am
      but one disappointment,
      one heartbreak,
      one lie away
      from being something
      that needs to be put back together.

mischief

Kiss me so I know
    your lips
    are capable of more
    than lying to me.

premonition

I feel tears coming before they even fall.
> Reminders of the sticky remnants,
> and evidence of hurt
> they leave behind cause my cheeks
> to act as a catcher's mitt.
> It's when they fall further down,
> and hit the floor hard,
> I face the fact of how
> it's not the letting go that hurts,
> it's the realization
> I should've left long before it began to
> that pulls me under.

a painting in vengeance

The first stroke was the most painful.
You opened my bleeding heart
and exposed my open veins,
splashing them on the blank canvas.
The next stroke was worse than
the first as you stripped me down
to the fibers I was once made of.
The third, fourth and fifth stroke
bore no story, no color, and no life,
as you put my pain on display
and left my dignity in particles of ruin.
The final stroke came
as you tried to paint the happiness
back into my eyes,
the light they no longer possessed.
You even thought the way you fixed
my smile would make it all better.
I was a masterpiece, your masterpiece
of what love no longer was to me,
what it obviously was for you,
trapped in a body for everyone
to gaze upon, mock, and critique.

the debt for happiness

Goodbyes last longer
      than broken hearts,
      which is why I try
      to carry you with me.
      I desperately want to keep
      a piece of you tucked inside me,
      but happiness demands
      I let you go.
      It's the price
      I must pay for freedom.
      It's debt I owe, so I can smile again.

the natural bridge

It's so easy
>to gravitate towards you.
>The way your hands
>caress my skin causes
>my insides
>to stand at attention.

>The easy way your breath
>falls upon my ears
>makes me want to capture
>each syllable &
>every sound your words
>are compiled of.

>The penetrating glare your eyes
>stare into me
>forces my soul
>to hand you my heart.

>The natural way my body
>responds to your presence,
>convinces me this is the place

I've searched my whole life.

what we reap

I wonder if this is how she felt.
Did she lose sleep
when you were with me
and failed to return home?
Her heart, did it crack slowly over time,
or did it resemble
the abrupt snatching
from her chest like mine?
Were her tears heard
or did she suffocate them
in the softness of her pillow
like I do now?
Does the side of her bed,
where you once slept,
feel cold like mine now does?

It's 3am and I lie here, lonely,
wondering if she is somewhere
still feeling like I do,
still wishing you would come back.

late night vices

We gallivant throughout the night
> without a care in the world.
> I am caught up in this overwhelming
> affect your eyes pierce
> through my soul,
> as you ride the waves of my
> nostalgic hopes and dreams
> that we will one day mean more
> to one another.
> We hold onto the notion
> we are so much more than the lost souls
> we have committed to being.
> We know this fallible love
> is only lust and this moment
> like the many before will always be
> temporary fixes to tame
> our late-night vices.

purple is the sky

Love me with the kind of love
    that is mysterious,
    yet full of wonder.
    The kind of love that has
    never been wished upon a star,
    while conjuring
    a deeply rooted belief
    purple is the color the sky
    was always meant to be
    and you and I will live
    beneath it forever.

the taste of time

I kiss your lips
    and the saltiness from my tears
    soaks them.
    Your tongue
    taste like the last time
    we fought over her.
    The inside of your mouth
    hides your secrets,
    as the lies I swallow
    burn my throat.
    I try and fight through these feelings,
    but no matter
    how much time has passed,
    the bitterness of this heartache
    still settles within
    the lining of my lips.
    My mouth no longer remembers
    the good times,
    the taste of your love,
    and it saddens me.

do you ever think of me?

Do you miss me like I miss you?
  Does the axis your mind spin on
  even rotate anywhere near
  thoughts of me.
  Is it possible,
  I can be buried somewhere
  in the left hemisphere of your brain
  where our love
  would make sense to you,
  where you and I would be a
  more logical decision than you and her,
  or will I have to settle
  with being tucked away
  on the right
  as a simple fixture, a secret,
  a playful ideal,
  carved deep in the back
  of your imagination.

the problem with temptation

The problem with temptation
    is that all the roads lead to you.
    (they always lead to you.)
    The path of least resistance
    is not one I am acquainted with
    and although I know
    traveling down this god forsaken road
    will leave me broken,
    this time, when I leave, I will remember
    to collect the pieces of
    my sought-out heartache
    so, I don't find my way back to you again.

compromises

I smell of depravity
      and the death of love.
      My heartache befouls my clothing
      as I reluctantly
      wear it on my sleeve
      for everyone to see.
      My hands are hardened
      from holding onto our toxic love
      for too long.
      I want to let go,
      but the fear of being alone
      is heavier than his betrayal,

      so, I stay,
      and I wear it with pride.

the shaky sounds

Once again, I lie here beneath you,
      after I told myself I wouldn't.
      My nails dig into your back
      as your hands grip my ass.
      The black, empty space hides our faces
      as the walls try to smother the sounds
      that escape my lips.
      I know you want to believe
      I am fighting the urge to moan,
      to scream out in pleasure.
      But this room, these walls,
      and this darkness that covers us
      knows the truth.
      Internally, I am fighting a civil war
      between my heart &
      my unforgiving mind.
      And the shaky sounds
      are simply the tears of defeat,
      I refuse to cry.

reasons to stay

I lost myself trying to save you.
      I believed my love was enough
      to make you see how
      I was the one for you.
      I falsely persuaded my heart
      into thinking the gold coveted
      between my thighs was all I needed
      to make you come home at night.
      I wore the scars
      you proudly left on my face,
      hoping you would see
      I was loyal to this thing we shared.
      I foolishly manipulated myself
      into believing the tears I cried
      would echo throughout your ears
      and you would eventually love me
      enough to stay.

lies you tell on our pillows

It's the place where you whisper to me
      promises of forever,
      and I lie next to you,
      pretending the sound of them
      does not pierce my ears,
      convincing myself tomorrow
      they will mean something,
      and they are more than just secrets
      to be kept by our pillows.

eight months after

I've written this love letter several times
      since you left,
      and I never seem to get it right.
      It's eight months after forever
      turned into goodbye,
      and I am still sitting here
      filled with all the things
      I never had the chance to say.

where we hide our wild things

Tucked gently behind my rib cage,
my wild part beats hard and loud.
Coveted deep in the belly
of this unruly stature is a soul
that dances without reason.
Strategically planted inside
the bones of my restrained legs
is a passion that is slowly boiling
to the surface.
Buried beneath the skin
of this complex being
is a controlled circus act compiled
of all my hidden wild things
and you have no idea
how a simple touch from you
sets them free.

internal orgasms

He arouses the orifices
    that triggers my insides
    to come alive.
    He entices the monarchy
    of organisms
    concealed beneath
    the layers of my skin.
    He makes me ache in places
    love often circles.
    He makes my soul come.

all of the nameless

Every night, when I close my eyes,
    I see them all.
    Their faces drained of life
    and their empty eyes,
    a clear reflection of their souls.
    Their hands worn
    from the burden of my heavy love.
    Their ribs exposed,
    for me to see my name tagged
    on the walls of their hearts.
    They stare back at me,
    and for a moment, I travel down memory lane.
    For just a second, I let them know
    it wasn't meant to be like this,
    I fought to love them as best as I could.
    And though we can no longer be,
    I will always carry them with me.
    The nameless ghosts with bruised egos,
    faces I cannot forget,
    the loves I had to let go.

maybe you knew

I part my lips to beg for your forgiveness,
      but you press your finger
      gently against them.
      Maybe you knew,
      I was one lie away from
      breaking your heart (on repeat).
      Or perhaps,
      somewhere inside of you,
      you could see
      I was an unraveling tragedy
      in the making.
      If only I could've seen what you saw.
      I couldn't see it, but you knew all along,
      I was good enough for you.
      I wish I had grabbed hold
      of the faith you had in me,
      I should've fought harder to be that person.
      Maybe you could see
      all I needed was to love myself.

focus

How is it that you never noticed
        you were slowly killing me?
        How could you not see
        the hole in my chest
        from where you ripped my heart out.
        Can you not see the particles
        from my chest cavity beneath your
        fingernails—
        skin dangling as if I never mattered.
        Do you not feel my warm blood
        that has now turned cold,
        saturate your hands.
        Is this last gasp of oxygen
        not enough to show you,
        you were all I needed to survive.

whitewashed dreams

I've washed this dream clean
    time and time again.
    Purged you from the crevice of my frontal lobe,
    and the dark corners of my temple
    harboring those good times
    I hold on so tightly to.
    I've drowned my thoughts
    within bottles of forget me nots,
    but no matter how many times
    I try to erase any trace of your existence,
    my heart paints the memory of you
    across my mind all over again.

planted in pain

I'm tired of falling in love
    with hearts that belong
    to someone else.
    Heartbeats I am only able
    to listen to for a fragment of time.
    Love I eventually have to return.

heal to tow

I keep looking to you for something
I know you are incapable
of giving me.
I try to convince that girl
inside my head, head over heels for you
this isn't the only place love will find us.
But I hopelessly, cling to your vacant promises.
Expectations are the gateway
to a broken heart,
and I know the longer I stay here
hoping you will eventually
become what I need,
the longer I hold onto to
these unrealistic dreams
I need to place on the curb
with yesterday's trash,
the harder heartache will
press it's heel against my neck.

a house so empty

Each night, we lie here
> next to one another,
> breathing,
> existing,
> silently screaming,
> falling out of love,
> and I have never felt
> more alone.

tell me where hope lives

Tell me where hope lives,
    and I'll run
    as fast as I can to find her.
    Tell me how much it will
    cost to feel alive again,
    and I will barter
    a piece of my soul.
    Tell me she can make me whole,
    and I won't look back.
    I won't kiss him goodbye.
    I won't give her any reason
    to think my desire to let him go,
    is not real this time.

a carnival of heathens

The faith I had
> in temporary forever's
> were always
> my weakness.
> They were always the last step
> into self-destruction,
> and the heathen voices
> in my head
> would often remind me
> of this every time,
> I gave into you
> and you disappeared.

naked as the name

Undress me.
        Strip me of everything
        that reminds you of him.
        Wash me clean so
        I can be as pure
        as the day, I was born.
        Peel me back,
        layer by layer
        until you find
        where he buried the hurt.
        Unveil all of my brokenness,
        rip out the insecurities,
        and then,
        when you have found my core,
        fill it with your love.

soundless downpours

I sought refuge in my pillow.
      I harbored what I was feeling
      to protect the sanity
      that was escaping me,
      to protect your ego that was always
      on the edge of fragility.
      And even though you caused them,
      I started suffocating my tears
      since you never cared to hear me cry.

no one arrived

I waited for months,
      but there was nothing.
      To entice their return,
      I ripped open my chest,
      hoping the echo of my
      erratic heartbeat against my ribcage
      would pull them back in.
      I tried to stop breathing
      as if the silence would prove
      I needed them to survive,
      still none of them came.
      Not one of them arrived
      to fix what they had left broken.

sleeping with the lights on

I sleep with the lights on
      because I am afraid
      if I grant you one ounce of darkness,
      one opportunity to slip away,
      you'll abandon me
      like all the others,
      and I'll be forced
      to face heartache alone
      come morning.

false god

I idolized this love.
Recklessly, placing it on a pedestal
it was unworthy of.
I gave more of myself than
I should have,
thinking you would fall in line
and do the same.
I expected more from you
than you ever stated
you'd give and now
I'm scrambling to find a way
to believe in love again.

mood swings

Sometimes,
> I want to straddle love.
> Grip it with my thighs
> and give it the ride of its life.
> Then other times,
> I want to hold my middle finger
> up in the air
> and say fuck love.
> The things you do to me
> and these unpredictable emotions of mine.

2 centimeters

There is a bullet
>   with your name on it,
>   lodged 2 cm from my heart,
>   and I'm afraid if I attempt
>   to exhale
>   even the slightest ounce of you,
>   if I even consider a life
>   without you inside of me,
>   you will end me.

trip wires and scotch tape

We keep falling back together,
>tripping over denial,
>codependency,
>bullshit,
>and I keep breaking
>a little more every time.

i know better now

The longer I leave this door open,
    the more you feel
    it's okay
    to keep walking in
    & out of my heart
    and I can't keep being
    an open house for this addiction
    to kick it's feet up and stay.

layoff

I used to believe in forever
  until he showed me to the door.
  Confirming our love was now over
  and he no longer
  had use for my heart.

perspective

Maybe it's only meant
      for me to love you
      with half of my heart.
      Because maybe for you,
      all of it is just too much
      or could it be its meant
      for me to save half for myself?
      Because perhaps,
      it is me who can't handle
      giving it all away.

I don't know...maybe.

steady

My heart had always
been a wanderlust place
full of adventure and freedom.
Then you came along
and gave me a reason
to finally be still,
reaffirming it was okay
to plant some roots,
proving that a regular heartbeat,
was better than the rollercoaster
mine was accustomed to.
Even when I wasn't looking,
you gave me hope that love always
had a way of finding me again.

provoke

Entice my thoughts
    with such potency,
    you leave
    my soul envious
    and my heart
    intoxicated off your words.

misstep

There is a possibility
        without trying,
        you may inevitably fall in love
        with me,
        you're going to relinquish
        a piece of yourself
        that you may never see again,
        and all I can say to you is
        be careful.

permission

He asked for my heart,
    so, I handed it to him
    in hopes
    he would take better care
    of it than I have.

hoarder

I am collector of fragile things,
  broken things,
  one of them being you.
  And against my better judgment,
  I have somehow
  swayed myself into thinking,
  I can make you whole again.

serendipity

All I want
      is to touch the sky,
      and feel the stars tingle
      between my fingers
      and the moon
      to kiss my skin
      with its light,
      something more impossible
      than loving him.

crush

I fell in love
     with the parts of you
     I wanted to see.
     And it's possible
     those are the very illusions
     that keep breaking
     my heart.

certainly, not me

Who gave you permission
to rearrange me?
To crack open my rib cage
and touch the corner
of my soul where my heart
had given up on,
and darkness now covers?
Why would you willingly
fall prey to this madness,
when you know
I am incapable of love.

collector's item

I should've warned you
      my outer frame
      was nothing more than a disguise
      for the broken pieces of
      all the others
      who came before you,
      hidden beneath the surface.
      I wanted to tell you
      I was a hub for lost things,
      and if you stayed
      you would become a part
      of the many broken hearts,
      I housed next to mine.

caught between a rock & a hard place

I love someone
> who doesn't exist anymore.
> He died with the love we shared
> and buried out back.
> Still, I'm going to keep holding
> his hand.
> Maybe, he will find his way
> back to me
> before my heart realizes
> he's gone for good
> and gives up on this love.

willpower

My heart finally beats
    like it has something to live for.
    It's thunderous roar
    slams hard against my chest,
    and the echoing sound
    is harmonious to my ears.

momentary highs

Please,

just stay with me.
Hold my hand and let me feel
this counterfeit moment
that appears to be love,
for however long it will last,
before it slides through my fingers
and you walk away forever.

can't love me

He keeps telling me that
        he loves me,
        and I keep finding ways
        to refute him.
        One of these days,
        I'm going to believe
        he really loves me
        and with any luck,
        he won't prove me wrong
        and walk away.

lost cause

I know our time has passed,
    though you can't seem to come
    to terms with it.
    We missed our opening
    and trying to make this work,
    no longer seems worth it.
    But we'll keep trying
    with the crazy notion
    we will prove the doubters
    and naysayers wrong,
    the people that look and sound like us.

ignorance is bliss

If only I'd paid attention
    to the first red flag,
    or maybe the second,
    or third one,
    shit the hundredth flag,
    you waved proudly in my face.
    I wouldn't be here,
    picking up the scattered fragments
    of my heart, another time
    I cannot even begin to count.

moment of silence, please

Did you even grieve for us
    and what we now know is the end?
    Did you allow your heart
    time to mourn,
    the loss of this love?
    Have you even shed a tear
    for the years we've wasted,
    or is the moan
    caught in the back of your throat
    that she slowly pulls out of you,
    the closest thing I will ever get
    to a cry?

sweet talker

I'm a woman, easily swayed
    by a man with kind eyes
    and a soft smile.
    The kind of man
    who could draw me in
    with a seductive look
    and words full of charm,
    leaving me longing for more.
    The kind of men that have
    their intentions, the side effects to them
    disguised by desire.
    Those are the kind of men I fall for,
    the type that hide their deceit with
    linguistical nectar.

lovers anonymous

Heartbreak keeps showing up
    to this confession,
    but she doesn't realize
    guilt has already beaten
    her rotten ass to the party.
    She doesn't know blame has already
    sold me out and the scavengers
    are picking away at my dirty secrets.
    No one has told her that
    the 1,095 days, 65,700 minutes,
    and how ever many seconds I've been clean
    have all been thrown away
    for one more kiss, one more night with him.
    So, wait your turn bitch,
    there's plenty of dysfunction
    and relapse of mine to go around,

    I'm an addict.

the worst kind of love

I have these two hands
> to collect the pieces
> of my broken love
> I know you will mishandle.
> And knowing my history,
> knowing the self-restraint
> I can never seem to find,
> I will give it back to you
> just so you can do it all over again.

séance

I freed them all.
    I cut myself open up and I waved sage
    through every ounce of my heart.
    I set fire to my soul and screamed
    until they all left.
    All the ghosts of my past loves,
    walloping in the corners
    of my heart.
    All the monsters, scaring away
    any resemblance of new love.

a question that bleeds

I keep cutting this question
    of how, when, and where
    did we go wrong.
    Dissecting it as if
    the end results
    will be any different
    from the times
    I answered it before.
    Pulling it further apart,
    than the hole in my heart.
    Hoping the answers
    will bleed differently
    than what I now feel.

misdirection

Sometimes,
    we love the idea of love
    rather than it's truth,
    even when love itself
    is not there.
    That's what told myself,
    every time my heart wanted
    to believe you when you said,
    "I love you."

truancy

I can't keep fighting for
    a love
    you are no longer
    present in
    or even willing
    to show up for.
    It's time I skip out as well.

hopeless romantic

Why do I keep finding hearts
      more cracked than mine?
      Hearts, I know are beyond repair,
      and far more damaging
      to the care of my own.
      Is there a reason love keeps
      ending like this for me,
      when all I've ever wanted
      was to wake up with my arms
      wrapped around it, around him,
      when all I've ever wanted was to
      believe love really does end with
      smiles and sparkly eyes.
      Why do I keep looking
      for lost souls to save mine,
      when he hasn't seen his in a long time.

taking bets

He swears he loves me.
       He promises me forever
       as we drink bottles and bottles
       of temporary tonight's.
       But he doesn't know
       love has never been fair to me.
       He doesn't know girls like me,
       never end up with guys like him.
       He has no clue that girls like me
       will only break him into two.
       I will give him some time
       to come to his senses.
       I will give him just enough time
       for the infatuation to wear off,
       and for him to see
       he doesn't love me and leave
       like they always do.

nine lives

How many lives
>will I have to live
>before love comes to see
>all I needed was one.

confession

The most frightening omission
      I could ever admit
      to myself
      is that I knew
      you were no good for me,
      and I continued
      to dive head first into
      disappointment.

treehouse

Love is both
>   my safe place
>   and my weakness—
>   my shelter and my prison.

got a broken heart again

We've been here before,
> and each time,
> you make heartache
> look like something
> I could never live without.
> You love the hurt more
> than you love me.
> All the while
> I suffer in the
> most beautiful way.

let them leave

There is nothing more
        excruciating than loving someone
        who doesn't love you.
        No pain is more agonizing,
        than being so deeply
        engulfed in that love,
        you drown in it alone.
        So, when they say,
        "they've fallen out of love,"
        let them keep falling.
        When they tell you things that
        no longer feed your soul,
        don't fight for them,
        don't fight to hold to onto
        that kind of love.
        Because the truth is,
        they left long before they
        found the strength to even say it.

tragically beautiful

Just once,
>I want to be
>the happily ever after
>people
>really find,
>and not the love story
>gone wrong.

>Just one time,
>I want to write
>a poem
>that doesn't end
>with me
>wiping away tears.

this is me letting you go

I am numb
      and although
      I am alive,
      there are parts of me
      that would disagree
      with that very notion.

he wants to be a poem

I wrote another poem
>   about you,
>   about us,
>   and the thing that is
>   plaguing me the most
>   is I cannot figure out
>   what to name it.

>   I cannot fathom
>   how to even put together
>   the right letters to describe
>   what we were and it hurts.
>   So, I'll write this poem
>   about you,
>   about us,
>   and you can name it
>   whatever you like.

i'm sorry i wasn't good enough

You always found a way
    to highlight all my flaws.
    Despite your criticism,
    I fixed myself up
    and you still couldn't tell me
    I was beautiful.

    You picked and picked me apart,
    until I had no choice
    but to take a closer look
    at myself,
    at my decisions, at us.

    When you finally
    stripped me to my core,
    I put *me* back together again.
    Now, I am perfect for someone
    who will know I am good enough
    just the way I am.

boundaries

You want to be with me,
> but I can't be with you.
> I shouldn't need you,
> but you can't seem
> to live without her.
> What we choose to be
> and what we truly are
> continues to be separated
> by the invisible line
> heartache has drawn
> in the sand.

breathing underwater

I'm fighting for dear life.
    Fighting to keep us alive,
    but you are giving up.
    You are not trying to save us.
    You have no desire for our survival.
    You are the anchor,
    and I can't keep breathing for
    both of us.

    I can't keep breathing underwater.

suitcase

I think I'm going to unpack
     my heart this time.
     He seems like a safe place,
     and I've carried it around
     in this worn suitcase for far too long.
     It's been thrown, dropped,
     and mishandled more times
     than I can count.
     It's had its fair share of pain
     and it has grown tired
     of the instability,
     moving from place to place brings.
     Though I am leery,
     he seems like a safe place
     for me to reside.
     This time, hopefully is the last time
     I'm going to unpack
     my heart and finally
     make myself at home.

delusions

I need you to stop invading
    my dreams.
    Stop imposing on my thoughts
    when I know, I am nothing more
    than a distant thought
    long forgotten,
    as you lay next to her.
    Leave my lonely nights
    alone and let my broken heart
    mourn in peace.
    There is no need for me
    to relive the grief
    of you leaving me night after night.
    I can think of no reason
    for me to bury
    the memory of you over and over.

    One death is enough for one lifetime.

cautionary tale

We've been programmed
        into believing finding your soulmate
        is the end goal, the ultimate goal.
        This is what defines
        true love and without this person,
        you and I don't measure up,
        and will unequivocally be alone.
        But we're miserable
        in this invisible prison
        society has trapped us within,
        and it's only going to get worse,
        so, you might as well save yourself.

glimpse

I'd settle for a piece of you.
      A speck of any kind
      to prove there is hope for us.
      Anything that would appear
      we have some,
      any kind of love.
      That way I don't have to face
      my heart one more time
      with a look of defeat.

i'm just going to lie & tell you starting over was easy

I was going to create

    this extravagant story so you

    would think my heart has healed,

    and I was living this great life.

    I intended to fabricate this

    fictional tale of a great love I had found so,

    I didn't have

    to keep pretending my heart

    hadn't removed itself,

    and is still sitting in the palm of your hand.

    I was going to convince you

    my heart and I have moved on,

    so I don't have to face

    the truth of we haven't, but I can't.

    One day it's going to be true.

    Someday, day one will be a mountain

    I climbed and conquered.

wasting time on temptation

Senseless seconds that wreak
    havoc
    on time as I lay here
    next to you, moments
    after I said I never would again.
    I keep giving you
    parts of my future I know
    I will never get back,
    in hopes I won't have to deal
    with the reality of now.

chasing secrets

I'm not sure if I'm in
        pursuit of you,
        or the feeling I get knowing
        I could never truly have you.

origin of bad habits

Our beginning and end.
 The start and finish
 to who we were
 is submerged in
 the bottle of whiskey
 I drink to forgive myself
 for loving you.

the horizon is not a line

I touched the horizon
    and it sat between your lungs,
    guarded by the hallow armor
    it needed to survive.
    It trembled
    beneath my fingertips
    as I stroked the
    lines that made up its walls.
    I touched the horizon
    and it is not
    a line drawn in the sky,
    but a boundary
    placed between you and I,
    love no longer dares to cross.

hell in the holy city

You touch me
  and I can't help
  but feel you align
  within my bones.
  Your attraction for me
  is covered in sin and my lips
  long for a taste of the hell
  submerged within the layers
  of them once more.
  My eyes burn as I gaze upon you,
  fighting the tears
  desperate to be freed.
  You've convinced me heartache
  is something I am would
  die without.
  A hell so beautifully enticing,
  how can you be anything
  other than holy.

like deconstructed origami

I opened myself up today.
I peeled back the deconstructed
corners of me,
fold by fold, edge by edge.
I never realized how much
of our story had been
tucked away.
I could never have fathomed
how much of our tragedy
had been carefully
tattooed in the crevices of my heart.

I searched for you
in those deep pockets.
I dug deep inside our chaotically, folded love
to see you hid
our disappointments
deep in its bowels
and you tried to put me
back together as best as you could.

sunday coffee & second chances

Forgiveness taste as bittersweet
      as the caffeinated drug
      that interrupts my thoughts.
      I'm trying to be better,
      a better partner, a better lover.
      As I stare into the cup
      of stale yesterdays,
      I contemplate how we are here once again.
      I mull over the fact that this internal
      battle between fighting for you
      and running away is never-ending.
      I am trying to be a better lover.
      I keep telling myself it won't
      always be like this.
      Another Sunday morning
      I am faced with sadness and regret.
      More second chances
      I am forced to swallow because
      they said this is what you do
      when you're in love.

dead language, or learning how to speak

I've been yearning for someone
    to come and resurrect
    this language I slayed
    some time ago.
    Ancient linguistics, my tongue
    has buried beneath its surface,
    and I no longer mourn.
    I've been waiting for someone
    to simply breathe life back
    into the walls of my mouth,
    so I can learn to speak of love again.

when the bottom falls out

I claw my way to the top,
but it seems far, you seem far.
And even though
you are right next to me,
the distance of me
falling out of your grace
seems unbearable.

I reach for you, but it's always
like you barely
graze the tips of my fingers.
I plead for your forgiveness,
but the sound never escapes my lips.

This is what it feels like
when all is lost.
This is what the end of something
beautiful becomes.
This is what love looks like
when you have given up
and the bottom falls out of my heart.

accidental birthdays

Every year the calendar notification on my phone
        reminds me of this day, your day,
        and as hard as I try, I can't erase it.

        Every year, I buy a card I sign, that I will never
        mail because I don't know where you've moved
        on without me.
        I rumble through the closet to pull out the gifts
        I couldn't bring myself to give you last year or
        the year before.

        This year, like all the others since
        you've been gone,
        I will send you a happy birthday text
        I know you won't respond to.
        I will put on that dress you loved and
        post a selfie I'm sure you probably won't see.

        Like last year, before the night is over,
        I will light candles on a cake
        that I will blow out with another
        hope you return wish,

I know will never come true.

I want to stop celebrating this day.
I need to forget the fact that another year
has passed and you've been given a
another chance to wipe away your past
and start over.

But every year,
the calendar notification on my phone
reminds me of this day, your day,
and though it doesn't know we aren't together,
I just can't bring myself to erase it.

the night we lost the moon to moths

I remember the crackling of wood
    as the fire's light
    competed with the stars.
    I remember how our shadows
    were finally free and we believed
    with this love,
    anything was possible.
    We lost everything that night
    and what we'd give
    to have a fraction of it back
    is trapped between yesterday and tomorrow.
    But no matter how bright the stars
    try to outshine it,
    the moon belongs to them now
    and we are no longer
    able to borrow its light.

flowers in my hair

The ray of sun hits my face
 as you slide the stem
 gently over my ear.
 For a moment, our problems
 have pressed pause
 and everything feels alright.
 Just for a second,
 the softness of the petals
 remind me of your touch,
 as the aroma of the flower
 distracts my senses from
 the unknown fragrance you're wearing,
 I know was left by her.

hiraeth

These feelings of nostalgia get the best of me
    and
    no matter how hard I fight
    to be free of you,
    I find myself longing for your embrace.

counting backwards from ten

Ten, nine, eight...
     times you tried to convince me
     I wasn't just someone you
     were passing time with.
     Seven, six, five...
     times we made love
     and I could feel her between us.
     Four, three, two
     occasions you called me her name
     and I brushed it off as
     a slip of the tongue.
     One...
     last time you told me
     I was your everything
     as I counted down
     to the days, she would take you back.

21ˢᵗ century bloodletters

You ripped me open,
>	stuffed me
>	with devastation
>	and sewed me back together.

Your name will forever be carved in my veins.

#yourefreeyourefreeyourefree

Time had always been
       our enemy and my saving grace.
       It was a distraction,
       until it tapped me
       on the shoulder to remind me
       people grow apart,
       people fall out of love, and
       despite my issues with being alone,
       people have the absolute right
       to be with whomever they choose.

       I won't hold on as tight anymore.
       I won't force you to breathe
       this air that is killing you inside.
       I'll swallow my pride and I'll let you go.
       you're free, you're free, you're free.

relearning happiness

Today is Monday.

It's a new week, another chance
for me to get up and give these sheets
I've harbored myself in a break.

I've given weeks to this bed.
Grudgingly, I have soaked my pillows
with enough tears over you.

Today, I am going to freshen up my smile,
and let the sun kiss my lifeless, deprived
melanin once again.
I am going to release these restrained
strands and give my hair
to the wind as it reminds me, I am still alive,
despite how I feel inside.

I am determined to look in the mirror,
I've shied away from and tell my reflection
everything is going to be okay.

127

Today, I'm going to give happiness another try.

games in which we rename everything

What is this thing this man has given me?
　　　This unknown feeling
　　　I cannot call upon,
　　　this sensation that causes me
　　　to scream out so loudly.
　　　I feel it pierce through my veins,
　　　stretching me from limb to limb
　　　as I adjust to his migration into my bones,
　　　his seizure of my heart.
　　　This is how good girls lose their souls.
　　　What could this blasphemous emotion
　　　I am unable to define be doing to me.
　　　Numbing the pain won't make it okay.
　　　Labeling it another name
　　　doesn't make it be something else.
　　　How come I can't say what it is?
　　　Why won't he let me call it love.

white noise

The voices attached to your memory
        cry out in my ear,
        and for once my heartbeat came
        to my rescue and drowned out the noise.

less like a flower, more like a sword

Nothing is as it ever seems with you
>and everything we knew to be no longer is.
>Love has become a sharp blade
>I keep throwing myself on top of,
>and it cuts me a little deeper each time.

balloons shaped like anchors

Exhale, inhale, hold it,
      then exhale again.
      Each time, releasing
      a little bit more of you.
      Each time, giving myself
      a fighting chance to survive.
      My lungs have carried
      the weight of us for far too long,
      and my heart
      has been the anchor
      unable to let go.

let's pretend i've never said this before

Let's pretend I never whispered,
    "you are my everything"
    or had the courage to say,
    "I love you" before.
    Let's make-believe the nights we've spent
    wrapped in each other's arms
    were nothing more than flashes
    of time owed to lust,
    days we wasted buried beneath
    the others' heartbeat.
    Persuade me into not believing forever
    was not your subtle kiss on my forehead,
    or your tongue holding my lips hostage.
    Convince me it was a lie when I said,
    "I've never been this happy."
    Tell me I never told you all of my secrets,
    so the breaking of my heart can be
    nothing more than a figment of my imagination.

surviving sadness

A bandage is placed over my heart
and stitches, roughly woven
through the tattered layers,
hold my lungs together.
I have caged the bruised pieces
of my soul, I feel haven't been
able to let you go,
so the rest of me can move on.
All of my moving parts
are slowly working again,
and even though breathing
without you hurts like hell,
I'm surviving this storm of sadness
that tried to take me out.

we told secrets in parked cars

Kissing,
> touching, moaning,
> fingers sliding against the moisture,
> as the steam covering the windows
> reveal the pleasure
> we place upon them.
> A confined location
> with evidence of longing, and maybe
> traces of love,
> left on top of the cool, leather seats
> as our bodies are flying
> from the high we are riding.
> We unleashed many secrets
> that night I fell for you,
> never whispering a single word.

ash in my veins

You blow on me,
and piece by piece,
I scatter into the wind.
There was nothing keeping
me alive, so I decomposed
into particles of a love
that burned to my core.
Now one from which I came.
Remnants of what remained
when we decided nothing
about this loveless union
was worth holding onto.
I found serenity in your leaving.
I discovered the purity
in which my soul felt in saying goodbye.
The wind owns me now.
Finally, my heart is free.

born a bastard

I am no stranger to being
    abandoned.
    No, I am most comfortable
    with this feeling of
    disconnect.

    Love,
    never cared who I was
    and I've been absent
    of it ever since.

how to eat honeycomb

Lick the tips, and only the tips.
Never too much, never too fast.
Slowly inhale me
and give me a chance to line
the insides of you.
Touch me softly, while cradling me
with a possessive grip.
I am fragile, sweet,
and good for you in the most sensual way,
but be careful with my heart
because we are a gentle madness.

your love is blue fire, red lies

In this life,

> we are fused together.
> I am floating, and you are sinking.
> Unable to let go of anything, while
> needing to be free of everything.
> Addicts of burning passion.
> Victims of overconsumption.
> We live for the nights filled
> with drunken madness, days
> that unraveled the truth
> behind who you were.
> We inhaled the lies
> as the smoke from this love
> would often cloud our judgement,
> diluting our perception of reality.
> Your love burned bright, cobalt blue flames
> as it bled, crimson misconceptions.
> And me, unaware of how unstable
> your love was, stood too close to
> the fire and you burned me.

wishful thinking

I don't know
what love looks like,
though I'd hoped for once
it had found me
and it looked
something like you.

sacrificial kindness

I want to kiss you,
    but that would
    only be
    something else
    added to the list
    of things
    I'd miss about you
    and regret in the morning.

a memory i cannot forget

I wrestle with the night,
      and the dreams of you
      that won't let me go.
      I'm trying to escape them,
      the memories of us
      that cling to me until dawn breaks.
      Déjà vu's of instances that may or
      may not have happened,
      but since I'm still sorting
      through what's real, what's a lie,
      the daydreaming disrupts my days,
      well into the night.
      I'm trying to forget you.
      My days are better when I'm not
      remembering you.
      My nights are easier when
      subconscious afterthoughts
      of you don't consume them.

      I will keep telling myself this
      until it believes me, until it forgets you.

calvin klein and menthol cigarettes

I still remember his smell.
>It was vintage, timeless—
>not like those fads that come and go.
>It would always cling
>to his skin, my skin,
>like a distressed pair of jeans,
>that fit you perfectly.
>Strong like a Virginia Red
>that intertwined itself
>within the hairs on your arms,
>unable to relinquish its grip.
>It mimicked how our love was.
>Strong and desirable,
>in the beginning, but as time passed,
>it became worn,
>reeked of an unpleasant stench,
>and traces of disappointment—
>leaving what was no longer good behind.
>I inhaled his toxic masculinity in large doses
>and unbeknownst to me,
>he did more harm than good.

But despite how much I've outgrown him,
I can never forget the way he smelled.
Classic, unforgiving, addictive,
embedded deep in the fabric of my skin.

all the things lost

love,

    the dream we all chase.

    Only to accept

    some of us

    may never actually catch it.

ghosts we no longer haunt

You have a portion of my heart
    gripped between your fingers,
    as you hold it for ransom.
    You leverage the possession of it,
    hoping will make me return,
    but I have no further use
    for the piece sitting
    in the palm of your hand.
    The part that is still lodged
    inside of me no longer has to
    sacrifice itself to keep that portion beating.
    It's not a part of me anymore.
    It's yours and it was
    all I had left of you,
    the last piece of unrequited love
    that was holding me back
    and now I can finally move on.

broken dolls

All I ever wanted
    was for you to feel like home.
    A secret place, life
    wouldn't dare come searching for me.
    A safe place, I could finally restore
    my long-forgotten heart
    the world was finally done pimping.

is forever real?

You are a perfect combination
of yesterday's
feel good moments and
tomorrow's bad decisions.
But I gave you a chance,
the last of my faith I had
to keep me from
turning my back on love.
I was hoping, just this one time,
someone wouldn't let me down.
I was praying someone could
make me believe again.

today it hit me

I should probably say my catastrophic downfall
      began the moment I started
      replacing my water with liquor
      to numb all the lies you told, but I can't.
      Nor was it when you
      confided in her that sparked
      my brutal war of insecurity.
      It may have been the first time
      I dismissed the hint of perfume
      on your collar, but I drank,
      and the memory disappeared.
      It could have even been triggered
      by the night I pretended
      to ignore the faint, imprint her lips
      left on your cheek, but I drank, and drank,
      some more until I forgot.

      I honestly couldn't remember the beginning
      of my reckless behavior, but then today,
      the truth slammed into me
      with a force I couldn't ignore.
      And if I had to guess,

if I were being completely truthful,
I'd say it began the first time
I convinced myself that all the wrong you did,
all the secrets you kept,
and lies you told me
were in the name of love.

tell me how to heal

I don't know how to stop hurting myself.
      I don't know how to plug this
      hole of self-sabotage I keep diving into.
      I'm here, I'm in the ring, and I keep fighting
      to hold your heart up, but the weight
      of you no longer wanting
      to be here keeps pulling us down,
      and I can't take off the gloves,
      I don't know how to stop fighting,
      I don't know how to tap out,
      accept this defeat and leave the ring.

love and other plagues

My biggest fear
>   is that you'll discover you
>   can be happy
>   without me,
>   and I will be forced
>   to live with this love alone.

to all the boys i've loved before

I'm filling up these pages with you,
    but how do I really move on?
    Do I let the memories of our happier times go
    when they still make me smile?
    Can I ever be free of the pleasure
    you left traces of between my thighs?
    Is there something to remove
    the sour taste of hurt you abandoned
    in the lining of my lips where your kisses
    touched?

    Do I ever stop writing about you?
    Will I ever not need the remembrances
    of you to tell my stories?
    Is me loving you
    something I have to live with forever,
    or can I finally leave them here for good?

    I've had an unhealthy addiction to you
    for years, and I don't know how
    to wean myself from you.

Maybe there is no end.

Perhaps, I will always love them.

the alchemist

Give me the kind of love
        I could never be rid of and carves
        a lasting impression on my heart.
        You are worthy of love,
        I deserve this kind of love.
        Spread my legs open
        and bury your soul
        in the layers of my womanly core.
        Forget about those
        who were there before you.
        They are nothing more than ghosts
        who no longer haunt me,
        fiends who are no longer deserving
        of the sweet nectar
        that sits at the corner of your mouth.
        Pour forever into my veins,
        as you pull out the sorrow
        housed in the crooks of my bones.
        Baptize me, bathe me,
        until you cleanse me of the hurt,
        your predecessors doused me in.
        Submerge me in euphoria,

and watch our love become
something god-like, something beautiful,
something magical.

die in love, live forever

At some point,
> we all become martyrs
> with our hearts
> cuffed tightly in our hands.
> Fighting the inevitable
> death that comes
> with falling in love.
> Hoping we find
> immortality within it all.

9780998148465